Of Heart & Mind
Poetry and Insights

Brie Metayer

Copyright © 2020 Brie Metayer

All rights reserved. This book may not be reproduced in whole or in part, stored in a retrieval system, or transmitted in any form or by means electronic, mechanical, or other without written permission from the publisher, except by a reviewer, who may quote brief passages, after informing the author, in a review or article.

Contact Author: AuthorLBM@gmail.com

First paperback edition August 2020

|Let's Be Miraculous Publishing, LLC|

ISBN: 978-1-7355021-4-4

Metayer, Brie.
    Of Heart & Mind: Poetry and Insights/Brie Metayer.

    1.   Poetry.

Printed in the United States of America

DEDICATION

This piece is dedicated to my mother.

I would not be who I am nor would I believe in my voice as a writer and poet without you. Thank you for all that you are, have been, and continue to be.

Brie Metayer

POEMS

Statement
Reflections
Centered
The Facts of Life
Rippling Effect
Inside Out
[Soul]utions
Unknown
Revelation
Absence
Peace
Within
In Syncopation
Embrace
Happiness
Royalty
Sands of Time
Connected
Tango
Caress My Soul
In[sight]ful Love
Horizon
Naturally Intune
To Be In Love
Four
Knowledge of the Senses
Here
Soul + Love
[Un]Conditional

POEMS

Shifted Meaning
Converge
Safe Guarded
Restricted
Reframe
Fear
Dark Forces
Stage Fright
Illuminated
Forging a Way
Embellishments
Depth
Unspoken
Lessons Planned
Knowing
It.
Light Fragments
Elemental
Emotions
Letting It Go
Sacred
Foundational
Freedom
Destiny
Perspective
Period.
Runneth Over

INSIGHTS | I AM

Introspection
Seek. Truth.
The Worth of Thyself
Focal Point
Attend
Who Are you?
Inner Knowing
En[light]ened Spaces
Expectations
Protective Factor
Identity
Glimpsing Within
Progress
Overcoming

Ascension
Exception[AL]WAYS
Searching
Comprehension
Expansion
Reminder
Timing
Just Be…
Ascend

Magnified
The Good. The Bad.
Re-Examination
Victimized | Root Causes
Lessons…
Fact Check
Bootstraps
Fragitlity
Limited
To Be Free At Last

Poems

Statement

No one can eradicate
your influence on this earth.
If anything,
they eradicate theirs,
as they extinguish their energies
on your efforts
rather than establishing their own.

However, with *you,* is where it begins.

Reflections

Looking within the depths of the soul,
perceptions of wells were
an accustomed truth.
As the search became stronger,
the mirage became visible.
Truth was revealed.
Oceans grace the land of existence.
The vision was distorted
by our own mind's eye.
Reflections of our own misconceptions.

Centered

Fine tune the self or graceful sounds
cannot soothe the ear.
Attune to self or intuitions
will be forever lost, leaving fear.

Resume to teachings
of past and present.
Daily occurrences are on course.
Flourishing beyond belief.

A new beginning
with each rising sun.
Warmth of life breathes
warmth of soul.

The Facts of Life

Deception only draws breath
in the company of ignorance.
If consciousness were to occupy the mind
to marinate and to flourish with time,
there would be no such thing
as villainous acts.

Consciousness is the kryptonite
to the sins of deceit.
If one were to fully understand,
this logic would rear defeat.
Honesty, thought, and generosity
can build the bridge towards unity.

Deception is the first domino to fall,
eventually bringing all that follow to doom.
It is the initial spark that lights the dawn
of a fiery and impoverished tomorrow.

Rippling Effect

Thoughts envelope me.
Gazing upon familiar features
reflecting from the pools below.

Fighting for tranquility.
Stillness.
Peace.
The ripples disfigure the images before me.

Racing against the tests of time.
Struggling to make sense of it all.
No one can stretch the waves.
Interconnected fates.

All we can do is wait.

Struggling remains in vain.
Patience until the calm graces the pain.
Virtuous in the interim.
Searching for a clearer view.

Eyes fall upon its reflection.
Observing the features.
Absorbing its essence.
Thoughts consume this empty space.

All we can do is wait.

Inside Out

Woven into the quilted history of our past,
we are forever connected.
Emotions run wild.
Tamed by experience.
Quickly we move among the stars
that acknowledges us with its twinkle.

Discovered essence, discovered paths.
Excellence unmasked.
Standardized beauty is all an illusion.
The greatness within is all the beauty
that matters.

Truth is…you're the universe, darling.

Embrace it.

[Soul]utions

Searching for answers
in the eyes of others,
trying to connect.
Attempting to recognize souls.

Searching within the depths of other,
while refusing to look into the mirror,
into the eyes we possess.
Still unable to connect with our own.
The center of our being we must first address.

Unknown

Pain of not knowing
can lead to confusion of the heart.
The past clouds the present.
A gift that often we regret.

A gift that brings understanding.
A gift that shapes us forever.
Discovery of self clears the path
to a story that continues to be written.

Hearts collide.
Love overrides.
Memories develop like old film reels.

Life unfolds.
New beginnings untold.
Find self.
Find love.
Find proof.
Find truth.

Stories of one,
Stories of us.
It all remains a culmination of words
that breathes life onto what has yet to be known.

Where do we begin?

Revelation

All this time I knew you could trust me.
I knew you could have faith
that you could place your heart
in my hands
and I'd always protect it.

Never did I consider
my faith in your ability
to protect mine.

All this time.
It never crossed my mind.
And that was part of the delay.

Absence

This silence,
Unlike peace,
does not settle the mind.
Rather, it unhinges it.

Peace

It cannot be given.
It can't be forced.
Peace is found from within.
Peace exists,
but it isn't recognized
by the ego.

Within

In my mind's eye
I see clearly.
Illusions escape me
understanding embraces me.
Open to the light of the world.

In my connection
there is only illumination
Completing fates design.
Fulfilling the purpose of the divine.

In my heart
I am filled with gratitude
beaming with the freshness of air.
Enveloped in the arms of love and light.
Expanding forevermore.

In Syncopation

It's like all the love songs
were written about our love as if they knew.
Rhythms of our hearts intertwine,
lacing the beats that accompany sultry voices.

Passionate words formulate
the many recipes of our love.
Extraordinarily.
Exceptionally well.

Who knew that we'd feel
the harmonious undertones
as our eyes locked?

Us.
Complex compositions.
Simplistic messages.
Love's truth.
In its truest form.

Embrace

Difficult in the approach,
Aiming to hold you close.
Hearts intertwine,
Plotting to plant the signs.
Skipping like an old CD.

Honesty in its significance,
Purpose in its form.
Nothing means more
than its abundance, its existence.
Claiming this space and renaming it ours.

What's yours is mine and mine is yours.
Collective visions.
Complementary efforts.
Embracing the journey ahead.

I am mine and you are yours.
Individuals separately.
Made in their likeness,
Whose rhythms withstand the strokes of time.
A masterpiece created.

Sublime.

Happiness

I can't make you happy.
No one else can.
It's all up to you.
All I can do is shine a light
on a happiness you have yet to access.

So, let's bathe in the sunlight, my love.

Royalty

We sit upon this throne,
gazing upon our kingdom.
Side by side entrusting one another.

Loyalty at its finest.
Presented to the world in unison.
Embracing the unknown.

Riches overflow in abundance.
They say everything has a price.
This is Priceless, I assure you.

It all means nothing.
For although they see the titles,
The only opinion that truly matters is that of
whom shares this home.

This throne we call our own.

Sands of Time

Memories crash against the shore of our life.
Wading back and forth with fervor.
A chill, a peace.
Washing over the sands of time.
Erasing footprints of imperfections
left behind.

Smooth over the crevices and make it anew.
Thoughts and words born from truth.
Affection and devotion season the water
that crashes upon you.
Vast and mysterious.
A familiarity that remains.

Wash over me,
cascading reflections of blue.
Limitless in its bounds.
Overflowing.
Renewed.

Crashing against the shore,
we watch as the memories wade.
Back and forth over the sands of time.

Connected

Chest to chest,
Feeling the warmth of your heart emanating,
Reaching out to greet mine.

Imprints of unique markings
placed upon my soul.
Closer to each other than ever before.

Speaking without words.
Comforted by the sound.
Beating hearts intertwine,
Making a rhythm that stands the test of time.

Tango

Reach for me.
Hold me.
Allow the warmth,
stimulated by our beating hearts,
to calm us.

Inhale.
Exhale.
Shield me.
Guide me.

Behold all that is in tune.

I reach for you.
I hold you.
Drums of love's wavelength echo in our
veins.

Inhale.
Exhale.
I shield you.
I guide you.

Love me.
I love you.

Beyond the physical.
Internal.
Earth defying.

Reach.
It takes two.

Caress My Soul

Caress my soul.
Understand my intentions.
Judge not.
Reflecting your desires.

Content in these efforts.
Voicing truth to these matters.
Extracting shattered pieces.
Planting new life.

Genuine concern for the wrongs of past lifetimes.
Protecting the light.
Letting it shine brightly across the lands.
Earthly bounds, but universal reaches.

Caress my soul.
Understand my intentions.
Judge not.
Together we rise.

In[sight]ful Love

It is through the lens of love
that we remember the beauty of life.
Comparing the likeness of our loves
to that of wonderful scents,
heightening our senses.

Lips as soft as rose petals.
Skin as smooth as silk.
Presence that breathes life,
the freshness of air.

Eyes that illuminate our souls
like the stars of the night sky.
A voice that rings in the ear
and penetrates the heart.

Lovely is their existence, their light.
To be in the depths of love
reminds us of the depths of the world,
our existence that we somehow see
at a distance.

Recognition

Your compassion.
Your heart.
Your mind.
Your soul.
Your being is beyond comprehension.

A rarity.
An enigma.
Souls connected.
Realization through the windows of the soul.

Ever present.
Protective force.
Understanding.
Fulfilled promises.
An alliance from this point forth.

Horizon

What lies beyond the horizon is a truth we
have yet to encounter.
Along this path, this journey,
it has never been crystal clear.

Mirages of expectations,
past hopes and dreams,
obscure our view.
Paths to join together
beyond the horizon
have never been clear or completely true.

But what lies beyond the horizon
holds much more than we could imagine.
Do you feel it too?

It may be a part of the unknown,
but it's a risk we shall take
for the beauty of truth that awaits.
Do you trust me?

Naturally Intune

To be the river that flows
along the land of man and beings.
To be the gleam of light
that shimmers and leads.
To be the frequency
that surrounds all that exists.
Everlasting source.

To Be in Love

In essence,
our long walk along a path built by faith
is based on trust and belief.
It is our belief in an existence that has yet to
be discovered, witnessed,
or even captured.

It is an experience that is only felt
when you finally step into its presence.
It touches your soul.
It sucks you into an awakening that you never
knew existed.

True, unselfish love does not lead to harsh
consequences,
but to awareness of self.
Therefore,
Being in love is not a blinding expedition,
rather it is a conscious endeavor.

Four

You are the spring
that quenches the need for innate goodness.

You are the flame
that illuminates the path and leads the way.

You are the ground
that holds the same weight of daily life,
keeping the balance,
the foundation of hope.

You are the wind
that whirls past the limbs of trees
and gently caresses the faces of many,
ensuring that sight is a limited thing.

You leave your mark for all to know.

You are essential,
elemental,
eternal.

Knowledge Through the Senses

With every breath,
modern day concepts, thoughts, and words,
The words of newborn teachings,
flow from my tongue
to the drums of your ears.

They beat down to the unique grooves
of your fingers as it fiercely taps against the keys
unlocking the eyes to a new awareness.

A new awakening.

Here

Here.
Holding onto the special moments
once shared.
Holding dear to dreams no longer near.
Hopeful at times,
Attempting to realize,
Nothing is for certain.

Hoping it wasn't all in vain.
Patiently waiting,
Patiently seeking,
Holding onto what could have been.

Here.
Searching through the landfills of 'what ifs.'
Standing upon the mounds of wishes.
Placing faith in the hands that
belong to another.
Outstretched.
Baring it all,
Awaiting the answers to come.

Here.
Unbeknownst to you and the legends that be.
Fixated on the possibilities.
The heart and soul aches.
Yearning to be held.
Grasping for the source of life.
Presently awaiting.

Here.

Soul + Love

Many confuse lust for love,
believing attraction encompasses the physical,
the all-consuming.
Believing that part is what takes the cake.

But darling,
there is so much more beautiful
and awe-inspiring
about that soul love.

The essence of one's being.
There is no distortion,
no burnout.

When you love from the depths
of their existence,
their truth,
you gain the universe of love.

Incomparable.

[Un]Conditional

Promises made in past moments
have guarded the ego for so long.
Illusions of fulfillment,
feeding condition in returned love.

Do for me and I do for you.
An exchange of wants and needs, too.

Where is the love
that showers from above,
and is limitless in its forms?
Receipts of exchanges, places, spaces.
All simple evidence of our mutually attracted
significance.

Where is the truth
that bursts from the heart,
relentless in its pursuit to be given?
Trapped by ego,
by selfish restriction,
expectation,
residence.

Release the shackles
of social inhibitions.
Expose the child-like wonder
of selfless compassion.

Let the corners of your lips
open its gates
to show the world your appreciation.
No longer must you restrain the love
you hold within,
Boxed in, held up,
and conditioned.

Release.
Expand.
Accept.
Unhinge.

Love without condition,
Undo the bounds.
For what you love,
will forever grow,
Unconditional in all its forms.

Shifted Meaning

Forever, Love.
Forever love.
Forever. Love.

Converge

Hand in hand,
Heart meets heart.
Colliding presence
And reflected pasts.

Part in part,
Life meets life.
Standing together,
Side by side.

Separate experiences.
Mind and mind.
Thoughts influence thoughts.
Familiarity with self and other.

Reflections of me,
Reflected to me.
Awakened paths.

Becoming one.

Safe Guarded

I know they'll catch me.
Always have and always will.

To the core,
I'm known.
Never escaping,
Willingly staying.

All wishes fulfilled.

Unknown to me,
all known to you.
That love thing is unconditional.

Unafraid.
Always a safe place.
No longer second guessing.

True forms and all their shapes and sizes.

Never fitting the mold,
ever changing.
Free falling.
Not a care in the world.

I know they'll catch me.
Always have and always will.

Restricted

We are conditioned to see complexity
as the most productive route.
 Simpler and clearer paths
are seen as too convenient and untrustworthy.

Somehow, we desire freedom
among the chaos.
Although always accessible,
it's too good to be true.

Never appreciating its roots.

Reframe

Part of our problem is that
we are fixated on time.
A constant competition.
A race to the finish.
Watching the time tick away,
Dreading the pain.
The pressure builds.

Are we done yet?
Are we there yet?
Why is it taking so long?

Treading along on the mill of life,
Focused on the time elapsed,
Versus the laps completed.

The journey, the distance,
is what truly matters.
How many miles?
How many steps?
Unfortunately, the journey is often seen as
irrelevant.

Focusing on the journey alleviates the
pressure
on the souls of the world
and the soles that greet the ground below.

Accomplishment of what is gained
versus the ticking time that no longer remains.

So, Reframe.

Misguided

Lost in translation of the soul.
Aiming for the codes to unlock it all.
Stumbling through the misconceptions,
Yearning for the gold.

Dimmer lights.
Complicated sights.
Searching for the treasure inside.
Coming into one's self.
A key that has yet to be found.

Fear

The warmth that lies
in the center of the heart had awakened.
It is then, you sense the unfamiliar glow
that oozes out of your pours and gleams
beyond your reach.

Shaking the walls you've built,
walls once barricaded
all to avoid humiliation
and lack of dedication.

However, falling into the depths of pain
was not the entire truth.

Although fear of uncharted territory
remained hidden behind the curtain,
What really awoke the fear
was that of accepting the peace,
of accepting the warmth and basking in the
solar rays.

Fear of being exposed to the elements
in case that happiness
were to be ripped away.

Ah, yes, it was not the fear of falling.
It was the fear of losing after allowing yourself
to bask in the sunlight.

Dark Forces

The past is only daunting, haunting,
when fear is deeply rooted within.

Misunderstandings.
Hurt in vain.
Awareness unlocks the door
to the boogey man.

But it is strength and courage
to open the door
that faces the depths
of the darkness.

It is only then that shadows
will be faced by the light
that creeps in from beyond the barrier.

Stage Fright

What do you hide away from the world?
What troubles your mind so effortlessly?
Bound by the chaos unintentionally.
Plaguing your spirit
and leaving you out in the cold.

Release it.

The veils of limitation of self
no longer serve you.
Relish in the greatness within.
Do not live behind the shadows
of your doubts and fears.

Hiding away your truest qualities,
Avoiding the critiques.
Step upon the stage.
Be ready.

They'll love you.

Illuminated

You can only recognize
the light in the darkness.

An enemy and a comrade.
Understanding and perspective
highlight the view.

With that of free will,
which do you choose?

Forging a Way

Brick by brick.
Construction commences.
Calloused hands embrace the process.
Labor intensive, but truly worth it.
A culmination of all that is and ever was.

A collective.

Embellishments

Who am I?
Who are you?
Strip away the added trinkets,
the jewels,
the masks.
Thinking of times of the past.

Shed the hurt,
the pain.
Shed the thoughts and perceived truths of others.
What is left?
What truth do you possess?
What message do you hold within?

Foundation.
Clean slate.
Where do you stand now in this world full of embellishments?

Depth

They talk about it,
but to experience it
is a whole other universe.

The deep crevices of the soul
guard truth of what is known
or soon to be so.

Internal guides often refused,
unbeknownst to the seeker,
blinded by earthly things.

Universal and Godly truths
are often grounded in the depths
of faceless and intangible things.

Shoveling down to the roots of self.
Seek.
For once you were lost,
but can be found in depths
of the entrenched.

Unspoken

One look.
One breath.
What breathes life into me,
Breathes life into you.
Love exudes from the pours of the beloved.
An unspoken understanding between two.

Lessons Planned

There is truth
and there is purpose
in the merging paths of our lives.

What lessons lie ahead and behind?
Be open to the teachings,
the ins and outs of love and life.

Answers are hidden therein.

Knowing

Cool skies.
Grey eyes.
Storms arrive.
In due time.
Calmness settles.
Trees rustle.

Droplets drum
against the tin above.
Peace?
Rage?
Painted views
only understood
by the few.

It.

It washes over you like a current.
Electrifies the mind.
The body.
The soul.
You decide what "it" is.
It all f[it]s within.

Light Fragments

I am a prism that captures
the light from above.
Reflecting all the colors that encompass me.
Exuberant in its likeness,
exclaiming the unique blends of a mystery, whose
journey only reveals itself
from the fragments therein.

Elemental

Raindrops gravitate toward the earth,
The place of the living.
Cleansing what was and
inspiring that of what is to come.

Emotions

They push against the stubborn debris
of broken branches,
urging to break free.
The pressure builds,
fighting a battle that seems to be in vain.
The strength only grows,
weakening the blockade,
and tearing it apart.
Flowing with vigor
until it meets with foreign grounds
that now feel like home.

Letting It Go

We've become enmeshed.
It's a way of being.
A relationship to the thing that hurts us most.
You want to change,
but it's hard.
I know.
It's scary to see what's on the other side.
But you have to.
It's the only way to grow.

Sacred

Hushed tones acknowledge its presence.
The gift of unoccupied spaces.
Acknowledging the light that beams from
within.

No need for apologies.
Precious life emerges.
No one can compare to
its grace,
its glory,
its grandeur.

A possession, it is not.
Enveloped by the galaxies above.
Whole and everlasting.
Dynamic.

It must be protected,
No questions or doubts.
Hold dear to the heart.
No other can compare.

Foundational

Trust the ground for which you stand.
Nothing grows, holds,
Unless intently planted.
Known.

Substance of life and light.
Planting a lifetime love.
Make peace with the pieces assumed to be
buried underground.

Dig deeper.
Work harder.
Strolls above mean nothing
if not on solid ground.

Freedom

When they see us, they say,
"someone finally locked it down?"
We say, "locked it down?"

Never.

Given the freedom to fly?

Always.

Destiny

There is no need to seek high or seek low.
Across the horizon,
there is no need to go.
What is destined to be
shall always come.

Free will is at play
and detours may appear.
However, the journey proceeds,
the calm blocks the fear.
For what is for me
shall always be,
my dear.

Perspective

Up above, the moon illuminates the sky.
Straight ahead, it reflects back to us.
Move a few feet and it seems
the moon changed its path.
Did it really?
Or do you only see the change
due to a different position,
a different point of view?
Remove self.
Now reconsider.

Period.

Souls. Connect.
Spirits. Eternal.
Signs. Everywhere.
Significance. Internal.

Runneth Over

When entering the journey of love,
your cup should be full.
The love of your partner
should simply add to this cup.
Your cup will runneth over.
Overflowing with adoration and devotion.

Filled with acceptance and abundance.
Swirling with care and affection.
Encompassed with respect and honesty.
Embodying love in its completeness.

Should your partner break from
adding to your cup, fear not.
Your cup will remain full as it once was.
There is no emptiness to account for.
Their love never compensated for the lack you
held inside, rather they added to the depths of love
that was and continue to remain in abundance.

They lose nothing by adding theirs
as you lose nothing by adding yours.
No expectations to fill
and no disappointment for inability to do so.
Giving without the need or want to receive.
It runneth over in the humblest and purest way.

Do not fill my cup.
Please add to me as I add to you, so our cups may
runneth over.
Forever.

Thought Process

What poems resonated for you? If you feel called to, write your reflections here.

Thought Process

What poems resonated for you? If you feel called to, write your reflections here.

Thought Process

What insights resonated for you? If you feel called to, write your reflections here.

Insights
Introspection

Seek. Truth.

> Seek to discover inner knowing.
> Strive to be open to new possibilities.
> Ever evolving conceptions and perceptions.
> What is truth?
> It is defined by the present knowing.
> The present you.

The Worth of Thyself

Once you discover that *all* that you are is worthy of your own love, then everything else no longer feels like a feat to overcome.

Focal Point

    Accept what is.
    Be open to changing perspectives.
    Speak in order to be heard.
    Enlighten yourself; enlighten your world.
    It all begins with the lens from which we see.

    No one else can truly change it, but you.

Attend

    Listen to the elements.
    Hear the rhymes of times that once were.
    Understanding lies there.

Who Are you?

> At your core is your *Truest* self.
> Not the labels and roles you've grown accustomed to.

Inner Knowing

If you know yourself, you know your truth.
If you know your truth,
you finally connect with your purpose.
It all starts within.

En[light]ened Spaces

> You have to learn to not expect from others
> but also not allow yourself to fall back
> and dim your light.
> You must fight for yourself.
> You matter.
> You deserve to have a space too.

Expectations

>Expectations are not always bad;
>However, once you alter your acceptance of
>self, due to unfulfilled expectations, you've
>falsely tied your worth to expectation.
>
>Much like others are not obligated
>to fulfill your desires,
>you are not obligated to exchange your worth
>for that of minuscule things.

Protective Factor

There is resiliency in self-reliance.
Seeking outside of ourselves
and our own abilities
will leave us lost along the path of fulfillment.

Identity

Who we are and what we do
are two realms of life.
What we do often changes, but
who we are at our core, does not.
Although we may grow,
our truest essence remains.

Glimpsing Within

It's never about the other.
Look within and you'll find the answer.
No amount of searching that happens
externally will help you reach your greatest
potential.

Progress

It is not measured by quantity.
It's the change you decided to make on your own.
That's the real focus of the change.

Overcoming

Truly embrace the orchestration of the universe.
Find peace within to start anew.
Trust in the process.

Now, what's stopping you?

Thought Process
What insights resonated for you? If you feel called to, write your reflections here.

Insights
Ascension

Exception[AL]WAYS

We are all exceptional.

Those who truly believe they are,
always see exceptions to forge their own way.

Searching

> Life is much like a scavenger hunt.
> You may not know where
> or what the answers are,
> but you know one thing for certain.
> The answers lie close by,
> awaiting to be discovered.

Comprehension

> The mind and the brain
> are not mutually exclusive.
>
> Much like love.
> Much like the soul.
> Much like consciousness.
> The mind can only be accessed through
> understanding.

Expansion

> Evolve. Be open.
> There's a higher purpose awaiting you. You are meant to achieve your heart's desire.

Reminder

>You are a culmination of
>beauty,
>intelligence,
>strength,
>and resilience.
>
>Shine brightly without limitation.

Timing

It's all a divine plan.
Not all are meant to understand.

Find comfort in that.

Just Be…

It cannot be forced.
Let it flow.
It's as simple as that.

Ascend

> Reach higher.
> Achieve greatness.
> You're a force to be reckoned with.

Thought Process

What insights resonated for you? If you feel called to, write your reflections here.

Insights
Magnified

The Good. The Bad.

>Are you only a good person
>simply because You are placed
>in comparison to those deemed as bad?
>
>If everyone were deemed as good,
>would You still think You were?
>
>Or is it placed on another scaling system?

Re-Examination

The trials of Life do not simply disappear due to the presence of love.

It simply tests it.

Victimized | Root Causes

> We criminalize the effects of the past,
> but don't reprimand what started it all.

Lessons…

How can one teach if one barely grasps the material to effectively execute?

Fact Check

> To understand means to know.
> But the opposite is not equivalent.

Bootstraps

You can tell someone to pull themselves from their bootstraps.
But not everyone has a pair of boots or even shoes for that matter.

Fragility

> Tragedy reminds us that our assumed
> invincibility and longevity of time
> are simply an illusion and a construct of our
> minds.

Limited

Never refuse to expand your perspective.
Otherwise, you may be placed
in larger spaces, but still feel stuck.
Lost in the shores
because you can see the barriers
holding it all in.

To Be Free at Last

The freedom to simply be,
is one of the most fulfilling
aspects of existing.

Thought Process
What insights resonated for you? If you feel called to, write your reflections here.

To all of the wonderfully made individuals who occupy this world, may this work inspire and renew you. You exist for a reason.
Embrace who you are.

      Peace & Love,

Brie Metayer

www.ingramcontent.com/pod-product-compliance
Lightning Source LLC
LaVergne TN
LVHW051524070426
835507LV00023B/3294